ATLANTIC CANADA

ATLANTIC CANADA

TEXT BY
HARRY BRUCE

PHOTOGRAPHS BY
DUDLEY WITNEY

KEY PORTER·BOOKS

Page 1:
Picturesque Peggy's Cove is one of Canada's most photographed and painted spots. This quintessential fishing village is a short drive from Halifax, N.S.

Pages 2-3:
The sun sets at Arnold's Cove, on the west coast of Newfoundland.

Page 4:
The lighthouse at Cape Bonavista, Nfld., has been restored to the 1870 period. The silver-plated reflectors date from 1816.

ISBN: 1-55013-268-7

Printed and bound in Hong Kong

91 92 93 94 95 6 5 4 3 2 1

Contents

The schooner Bluenose II was built in 1963 in Lunenburg and is a replica of the original Bluenose (1921-46), whose image appears on the Canadian dime.

Introduction

This intricate quilt is just one of the many crafts which can be found in New Brunswick. The Mactaquac Craft Festival in early September provides a good opportunity to sample a variety of crafts.

At fifty-six, I am celebrating my twentieth year in Atlantic Canada. My wife Penny, our three children, our black cat, and I were born in the richest and most envied part of the nation, but in 1971 we all moved away to the poorest and least envied part. We abandoned Toronto for the corner of Canada where the Atlantic Ocean coldly bashes four provinces, fog throttles the joy of June, the land sprouts rocks, and good jobs are as rare as politicians who don't make promises. Life down here is so tough that, for generations, people have been flooding westward to find work and wealth. Tens of thousands of Atlantic Canadians moved to Toronto. That's history. Torontonians, however, rarely moved to Atlantic Canada. That would have been madness.

My father, author Charles Bruce, was one of those same Atlantic Canadian expatriates. I grew up in the heart of Toronto with a man who talked, dreamed, and wrote about a place that was mysteriously *better*. He was born in a snug, white farmhouse in Port Shoreham, Guysborough County, Nova Scotia, and he injected all his poetry and fiction with his lifelong love of both the neighbourhood he'd left, and the sheet of moody ocean that lay in the south. He craftily injected me with some of that same love, and though I took a long time getting here, I now live and work in the house where he was born.

When I was eleven, he sent me here by train to spend all of July and August with my aunts and cousins from across North America. To a child, two summer months are half of forever, plenty of time for things to get a foothold on the mind, things like a chorus of birds at dawn; the gurgle of a tidal gut in mid-morning; the smell of hay and fir in the afternoon; cowbells at dusk; the distant sound of surf-sucked gravel late at night; and all day long, the laughter of the bluenose kids on the farm next door. I never forgot that summer, and came back to Port Shoreham again and again for more of the same.

When I was eighteen, my father banished me to his alma mater—Mount Allison University, Sackville, New Brunswick—to get a three-year dose of the Maritimes. I soon lusted after girls from towns with exotic names like Carbonear, Oromocto, Tignish, and Tatamagouche, and in the men's dorm, I shot the breeze with yarn-spinning, young jokers from Newfoundland, Prince Edward Island, New Brunswick, and Nova Scotia. Their accents sounded lilting, rural, almost foreign, and their cursing was more raunchy and ancient-sounding than any I'd ever heard at home. Moreover, it was impossible for a Toronto boy not to notice that both the girls and the jokers were fanatically loyal to their own hometowns and provinces.

Thanks to Mount Allison, I spent the most impressionable years of my life not only cocooned with 750 young Maritimers and Newfoundlanders, but also exploring east-coast Canada. On my travels, I wore my father's thirty-year-old Mt.A. sweater, a woolly, garnet-and-gold bum-hugger with a thick collar I could pull up to cover my ears. For hitch-hiking, that Joe-college garment was a godsend, and I did a fair bit of exuberant kicking around in the Maritimes.

Potatoes are one of Prince Edward Island's major crops.

The good times of my youth are therefore inseparable from

down-east memories: the smell of the pines and the ocean breeze at a Halifax park; girls I knew and beer I drank in Moncton; sailing for the first time on a sea-going ferry; and explosions of surf, wind-lashed marshes, ice-scraped barrens, fleecy mist on Cape Breton cliffs, sumptuous dunes on Island beaches, and everywhere, those white, green-trimmed farmhouses like the one at the old Bruce place.

I didn't get to Newfoundland until twenty years later, but when I did, a small miracle occurred. Just over the dark rocks of Signal Hill, at the capital city of St. John's, a wooden village lined a tiny harbour. This was Quidi Vidi, and in some respects, it had scarcely changed in two centuries. The entrance to the cove was a gut so narrow I could almost have jumped across. Above it sat a battery with four cannons, which tourists were allowed to fire in the summertime, and the whole aspect had the cosy charm (if not quite the warmth) of anchorages in certain West Indian islands.

On the November afternoon that I inspected the Quidi Vidi battery, the ocean wind was heavy with fog and cold rain, and I thought I was alone. I removed my glasses, dried the lenses with my tie, put them back on, glanced up at the soaking slab of black rock behind the cannons, and there he was, not thirty feet from me, as still and cool as a statue. A hulking snowy white owl. He looked at me as though I might be a mouse worth dispatching. I had never seen a snowy owl outside a cage, and his arrogant good looks told me once more why I feel better on the Atlantic coast than I do anywhere else.

The land of these four provinces was white man's first accessible wilderness in the New World, and south of the Arctic anyway, it may well be his last. The cannons and the wild, white owl reminded me that although the Anglican Cathedral in St. John's may indeed be one of the finest examples of Gothic architecture in the New World, my rented car might still collide with a moose only a few kilometres down the highway. More than anywhere else in North America, Atlantic Canada offers a satisfying mixture of wildlife and human history.

When New York City was still a Dutch village, the French built Fort Saint Louis just up Chedabucto Bay from where I'm now writing. The English captured Port-Royal (Annapolis Royal) at the other end of mainland Nova Scotia in 1654, and that turned Fort Saint Louis into the most important French settlement in all of what's now Atlantic Canada. Pirates from Boston pillaged it in 1688, but the French refortified it and installed soldiers. In 1690 two British ships bombarded it for six hours, then sent troops ashore to set it afire. The fort surrendered, and with a drum beating and a friar at their side, a handful of French soldiers marched smartly into captivity. Their defence had been so courageous that Governor Frontenac himself praised their commander.

That's a titbit of neighbourhood history. Now for the wildlife. Last summer, while great, blue, stick-legged herons stood in the nearby mud, my adult children and I climbed aboard our beloved centreboard yawl, *Moonshadow,* and pretty soon we were flying past the red-brick clock tower in Guysborough town, and out toward the breezy glory and marching whitecaps of the big bay. Just as we passed the summer bungalow that squats on the buried ruins of Fort Saint Louis, someone said, "Holy smokes! What's that."

A sleek, shiny hairless flank—as white as milk, and brilliantly sunlit against the royal blue of the bay—slid partly out of the water, and vanished. Then it did it again. And again. Then it blew spray into the air. With no motor running, *Moonshadow* was as quiet as our breathing, and she sneaked up to within a few metres of the gleaming beast. Then it was gone. It plunged toward the floor of the sea, leaving us gasping and laughing on Chedabucto Bay. Seals, porpoises, bald eagles, ospreys, ducks, loons, cormorants, and huge black-backed gulls were old stuff to the crew of *Moonshadow*, but this was the first time any of us had ever seen a beluga whale.

It seems to be the way of the world that human history must eventually plunder the wilderness, but meanwhile Atlantic Canada remains a sweet secret for people who enjoy both the owl and the fort, the moose and the cathedral, the whale and the town clock. My father knew that. Just before I left Toronto in 1971, he said, "I think you'll have a lot of fun down there." He was right.

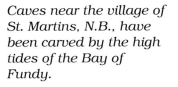

Caves near the village of St. Martins, N.B., have been carved by the high tides of the Bay of Fundy.

13

New Brunswick

*The remote Mount
Carleton Provincial Park
can be reached from
Saint Quentin, N.B.*

Rising a mere 821 metres, Mount Carleton was only a tenth as high as Mount Everest, but "it was there," and I had to climb it. After all, it was the highest peak in the Maritimes. "There" was in Restigouche County, up in the northernmost corner of New Brunswick, and one crisp morning in June, my wife Penny and I drove into the French-speaking village of Saint-Quentin, picked up some salmon sandwiches at the Queen Hotel—which also offered strip shows, a travel book advised, "but only during hunting season"—and drove our little gray Toyota over forty kilometres of gravel road to the foot of the mountain. We locked the car, and with the noon-day sun making our shadows short, started up the two-and-a-half-kilometre trail to the peak.

The final ascent was so steep we had to clutch at rocks to pull ourselves higher. Wheezing, sweating, wondering if I'd vomit, I vowed to quit smoking, and refused to look anywhere but upwards. The hut at the top was bare, brown, and grubby, but its windows faced in all directions, and when we got inside, we saw everything we'd come to see: glimpses of far, shimmering lakes, and strong rivers that tumbled away toward east and west; and ridge upon ridge of bristling green forests, stretching for county after county until they vanished into a hazy skyline. How many hundred bears were out there?

Bears were on our mind. Two mornings before, we'd heard some bear talk. We'd stopped for breakfast in Newcastle, where the Miramichi River surges toward the Gulf of St. Lawrence, and since the eatery was crowded, we invited an older couple to share our table. The man said he'd just read in the local paper that a black bear had become so accustomed to people that he amused himself by lying down on the Newcastle-Chatham bridge to cause traffic jams.

That's nothing, his wife said. She had a better bear story. They lived near Montreal now, but she was originally from the Miramichi, and whenever she came home, she knew that the river was "*the* spot on earth." Anyway, back in her girlhood she'd heard about this bear. Every year, when certain lumberjacks returned to their camp, the bear showed up to bum food. He got bolder, and he was a very nice bear. He learned to join the men at a counter in the mess hall, and sitting on his own stool, to eat his dinner.

I looked carefully at this amiable, guileless, and sensible-looking woman of about seventy.

"God's truth," she said, "and that's not all. He got to helping the men move logs around, just like the elephants in India, and when they closed up the camp for the season, he lifted the generators onto the trucks."

As we drove toward Restigouche country, with our bellies full of scrambled eggs and our heads full of the woman's yarn, it occurred to me that, of all the Atlantic Provinces, New Brunswick is most like Texas. Its tales are tall. Many of its people love country music, and the outdoors. Most are open-hearted and open-handed. New Brunswick boasts about its mysterious panthers, big tides, big forests, big sand bars, big river salmon, and if they're colourful, even its politicians. No province is prouder of its tycoons. Why, this is the country that produced Sir James Dunn, Lord Beaverbrook, the McCains, and K.C.

Irving and his boys. Every New Brunswicker knows that, compared to the Irvings, the Ewings of *Dallas* are pipsqueaks.

Late in the day of the bear-story breakfast, we reached the Madawaska Museum in the bilingual, pulp-mill town of Edmunston, hard by the Quebec border. We noticed a tiny, 19th-century lumber camp, under glass. A Michelangelo among whittlers had carved miniature horses, men, wagons, sleighs, and axes, surrounded them with trees, and arranged them just so. At the bunkhouse door, a bearded man in a checked shirt held out his arms to hug a bear who hovered before him on his hind legs. Another bear carried a log in his mouth, and a third stood by with his claws stuck in a stump. God's truth.

It wasn't till the next day that we sat on a rock atop Mount Carleton. We drank warm Coke, munched the salmon sandwiches in the sky-high summer breeze, and watched a helicopter patter towards us. The Acadian port of Caraquet was only 165 kilometres away, and we knew this was the very day it was expecting a visit from President Francois Mitterrand of France.Had he asked to see the highest peak in the Maritimes? Had someone said, "*Monsieur le president,* allow us to show you our magnificent forest, the very foundation of the New Brunswick economy, and the key to so much of its history?"

I got to my feet, and there on the breezy pinnacle of the endless wilderness, gave the helicopter my best imitation of a Charles de Gaulle salute. If the President of France was indeed flying by, I thought that he, too, should know something I've known for nearly four decades: when you're travelling in New Brunswick, just about anything is possible.

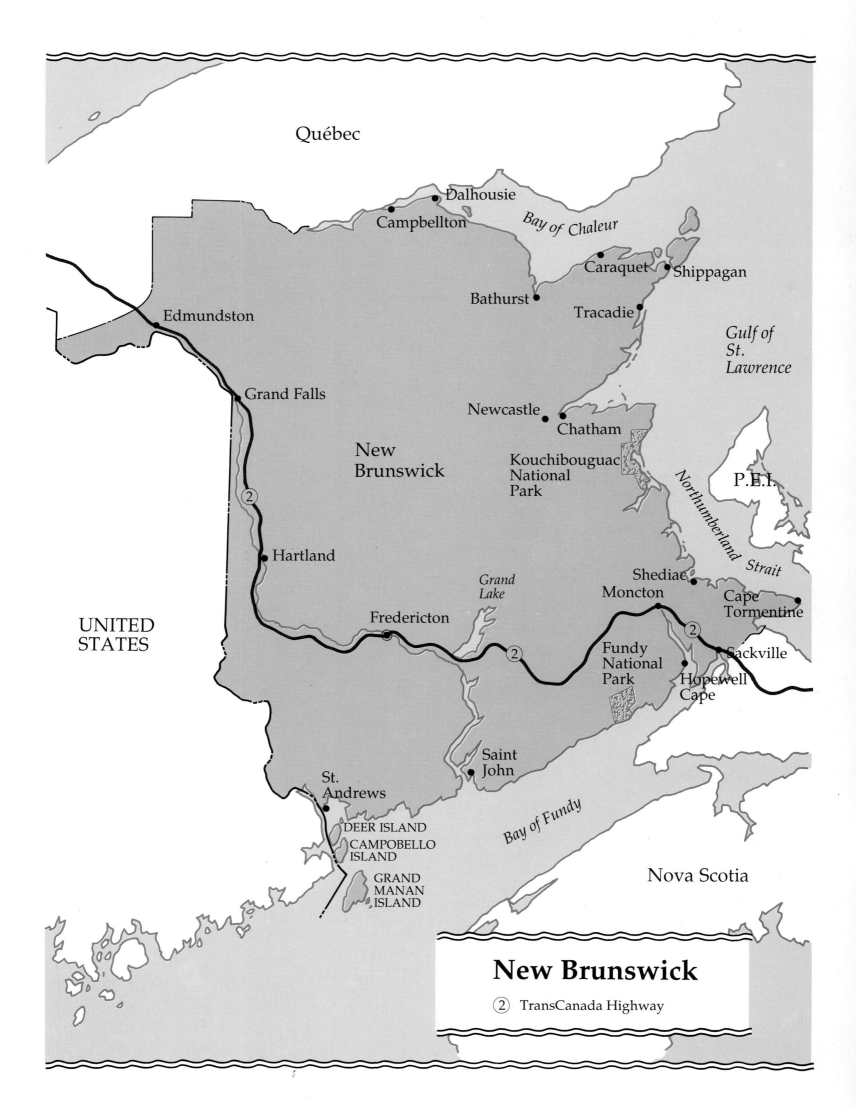

Québec

Dalhousie

Campbellton

Bay of Chaleur

Caraquet • Shippagan

Bathurst

Tracadie

Edmundston

*Gulf of
St.
Lawrence*

Grand Falls

Newcastle

Chatham

New
Brunswick

Kouchibouguac
National
Park

P.E.I.

②

Northumberland Strait

Hartland

*Grand
Lake*

Shediac

Moncton

Cape
Tormentine

UNITED
STATES

Fredericton

②

Fundy
National
Park

②

Sackville

Hopewell
Cape

Saint
John

St.
Andrews

DEER ISLAND

CAMPOBELLO
ISLAND

Bay of Fundy

Nova Scotia

GRAND
MANAN
ISLAND

New Brunswick

② TransCanada Highway

New Brunswick

Tourism New Brunswick
Box 12345
Fredericton, N.B.
E3B 5C3
Tel.: 1-800-561-0123

Area: 73 436 square km
Length of coastline: 2269 km
Capital: Fredericton
Population: 719,200
Flower: Purple violet

Fredericton and the Saint John River Valley

Fredericton, New Brunswick's capital, sometimes called the City of Elms, is situated on the banks of the Saint John River. The downtown area is a lovely place to walk, with the historic houses along Waterloo Row facing the river, and many notable buildings lining the main street. Christ Church Cathedral was the first new cathedral foundation on British soil since the Norman Conquest of 1066, and was consecrated in 1853. The Legislative Building, circa 1880, is a Victorian edifice which contains such treasures as a rare 1783 copy of the Domesday Book, portraits of George III and Queen Charlotte painted by Sir Joshua Reynolds, and a set of John James Audubon's bird paintings. Across the street, the Beaverbrook Art Gallery, endowed by Max Aitken, Lord Beaverbrook, houses many famous works, including the Salvador Dali painting *Santiago el Grande*.

The Playhouse, also donated to the city by Lord Beaverbrook, is the home of Theatre New Brunswick. The University of New Brunswick, one of Canada's oldest colleges, overlooks the city from its hillside setting.

Kings Landing Historical Settlement, west of Fredericton on the Trans-Canada Highway, is a reconstruction of Loyalist life in New Brunswick, covering the period from 1783 to 1900. More than 100 costumed "residents" go about daily life in the village's 60 buildings. The water-powered sawmill is one of the most-photographed buildings.

The world's longest covered bridge is found in Hartland, northwest of Fredericton along the scenic Saint John River. Spanning 391 metres, the bridge was built in 1899. There are approximately 78 covered bridges left in New Brunswick, most of them in the southern part of the province.

A bit further north (216 km from Fredericton) in the town of Grand Falls, the Saint John River drops approximately 23 m, creating one of the largest cataracts east of Niagara Falls. The gorge is 1.5 km long and has some interesting rock formations.

Saint John and the Fundy Coast

The oldest incorporated city in Canada, Saint John's first major influx of inhabitants came when several thousand Loyalists settled there in 1785. Now their descendants celebrate Loyalist Days in mid-July, and a Loyalist Trail through downtown Saint John leads pedestrians past such historic attractions as Barbour's General Store (restored and stocked to the years 1840-1940); Loyalist House, a Georgian mansion built in 1816 that pays tribute to the Loyalists; the old Loyalist Burial Grounds; a Jewish Historical Museum, and many homes and buildings that are worthy examples of various periods of architecture. Other important historical attractions are Carleton Martello Tower, a stone fortification surviving from the War of 1812 and now a National Historic Site; and Fort Howe Blockhouse, a replica of a 1777 blockhouse, which gives a panoramic view of the city. The Old Market (built in 1876) was modeled after the inverted hull of a ship. Many of the same families have operated stalls there for generations.

A unique phenomenon takes place twice each day in Saint John. The tides of the Bay of Fundy reach such heights that they force the Saint John River to flow upriver, creating the Reversing Falls Rapids.

St. Andrews, 96 km west of Saint John, is a lovely resort town which was founded in 1783 by United Empire Loyalists. Many of these early settlers dismantled their houses in Castine, Maine, and reassembled them in St. Andrews. Over half the buildings are more than 100 years old. The historic

Algonquin Hotel, whose turrets dominate the town's skyline, was built in the early 1900s.

In the western extremity of the Bay of Fundy lie the three Fundy Islands - Deer Island, Campobello and Grand Manan. There is ferry service to each one. Boat tours are available from all three islands. Off Deer Island it is possible to see Old Sow, the world's second largest whirlpool. Campobello was the summer home of President Franklin D. Roosevelt, whose 34-room "cottage," a red-shingled, green-roofed Dutch colonial mansion, is open to the public. Grand Manan is the largest of the Fundy islands and is noted for its craggy cliffs and picturesque harbour. A favourite with bird-watchers, Grand Manan was visited in 1831 by world-renowned ornithologist John James Audubon, who did many of his sketches there. Whale-watching, photography, painting, and rockhounding are popular island pastimes.

The coast of Fundy National Park shows the action of the high tides of the Bay of Fundy. Dozens of coves and inlets punctuate the shore of the park and are complemented by woodlands, inland lakes, and flourishing wildlife (approximately 219 species of birds have been sighted there).

The rocks at Hopewell Cape are possibly the most dramatic result of the mighty Fundy tides. These rocks have been sculpted into formations resembling flowerpots by the sometimes 16-metre-high tides.

Moncton and the Southeast Shore

Moncton is one of the transportation hubs of the Maritimes. With its mixture of French and English population and its recently-developed shopping, nightlife, and fine dining opportunities, the city is assuming an increasingly cosmopolitan character.

The Université de Moncton is one of the few French-language universities in the Atlantic provinces. The campus houses the Acadian Museum and Art Gallery, as well as the Centre d'Études Acadiènnes with its collection of documents, microfilm, and maps relating to the history of Acadia.

Two natural phenomena in Moncton are popular tourist draws: the Tidal Bore rushes up the Petitcodiac River twice a day; and at Magnetic Hill vehicles move backwards, seeming to coast up a hill.

The small town of Sackville, home of Mount Allison University, is a 53-km drive from Moncton. The pretty campus features Owens Art Gallery. Near Sackville is Fort Beauséjour, a national historic park. It is one of the few Canadian fortifications at which fighting actually occurred.

Shediac, slightly east of Moncton on the Northumberland Strait, is known as the "lobster capital of the world." One of the finest saltwater beaches in the province is found at Parlee Beach Provincial Park. During the summer water temperatures sometimes reach 24 degrees Celsius.

Kouchibouguac National Park is the largest in the province, and its 238 square km of forest, salt marshes, and beaches make it a popular camping spot. Sand dunes stretch along 26 km of ocean. Travelling north from Kouchibouguac on Route 117 brings one to Escuminac, where a monument by New Brunswick sculptor Claude Roussel commemorates the 35 fishermen who lost their lives at sea in 1959.

The Miramichi Basin

The Miramichi river is famous for its Atlantic salmon. Outfitters in this area can offer a variety of activities, from fishing and hunting to canoeing. The neighbouring towns of Chatham and Newcastle are the main urban centres of this region. Chatham's historical attractions include the restored Loggie House (circa 1879) and the Miramichi Natural History Museum. Newcastle was the boyhood home of the late Lord Beaverbrook. His former home, now the Old Manse Library, contains many volumes from his personal collection, including some first editions. Nearby, at Bartibog Bridge, the MacDonald Farm Historic Park recreates a typical working farm of the 1830s. It includes an impressive stone manor house, outbuildings, fields, and orchards.

The Acadian Coast

When France lost the struggle for the land called L'Acadie (southern New Brunswick and Nova Scotia) in 1755, England ordered the deportation of the French in this area. Many of these Acadians escaped to northern New Brunswick to live in freedom. The Acadian heritage is still strong in this corner of the province.

Caraquet is known as the cultural capital of Acadia, and each August the Acadian Festival demonstrates this. Festivities include the Blessing of the Fleet, where as many as 60 boats, all decorated with flags and ribbons, are blessed by the bishop of Bathurst. A wide range of Acadian entertainment such as sporting events, parades, and dances follows. Near the Caraquet wharf, the Acadian Museum portrays the history of the local people. Just outside Caraquet, the Acadian Historical Village recreates the lives of Acadians between 1780 and 1890.

The Restigouche Region

Campbellton is the first New Brunswick city many travellers encounter as they cross the bridge from the Gaspé Peninsula in Quebec. Situated at the western end of the Bay of Chaleur, Campbellton is an important outfitting and service centre for the sports fishermen who come from all around the world to fish for Atlantic salmon in the famous Restigouche River. Sugarloaf Mountain, a volcanic mass 283.2 metres high, stands at the back of the city, and Sugarloaf Provincial Park has an excellent ski hill and lodge.

Mount Carleton Provincial Park is accessible from Saint Quentin. This remote park offers a true wilderness setting for a wide range of outdoor activities including fishing, boating, bird-watching and rockhounding. There is an extensive network of hiking trails in this park, including one that winds its way up Mount Carleton, providing a spectacular view from the peak which, at 821 metres, is the highest in Atlantic Canada.

Low tide in the Bay of Fundy reveals striking geological formations at Mary's Point in southeast New Brunswick.

*Colourful boats are
moored at Dipper
Harbour, N.B.*

Lobster traps line the Bay of Chaleur, near Jacquet River, N.B. The hills of the Gaspé Peninsula can be seen across the water.

The giant lobster in Shediac, N.B., symbolizes the town's reputation as "lobster capital of the world."

The Hole-in-the-Wall is just one of many landmarks found on the various nature trails on Grand Manan, N.B., the largest of the Fundy Islands.

Interesting rock formations make Heron Island, N.B., in the Bay of Chaleur, a rewarding trip for artists and photographers. It is accessible by boat from New Mills.

A unique phenomenon takes place twice a day in Saint John, N.B. The tides of the Bay of Fundy reach such heights that they force the Saint John River to flow upriver, creating the Reversing Falls Rapids.

A boat stranded during low tide, near Rockport, N.B., illustrates one consequence of living near the highest tides in the world.

A farmer at Kings Landing Historical Settlement, west of Fredericton, N.B., works his land as Loyalists did a hundred years ago.

A fisherman tries his luck in the Miramichi, one of several famous salmon-fishing rivers in New Brunswick.

Expressing pride in their heritage, many Acadians decorate their houses during village festivals. The Acadian flag is a common sight in northeast New Brunswick.

The Acadian festival in
Caraquet, N.B., begins
with the Blessing of the
Fleet. As many as 60
boats, colourfully
decorated with flags and
streamers, are blessed
by the Bishop of
Bathurst.

Stately buildings line the street to the harbour in Saint John, N.B. This city was first settled by several thousand Loyalists in 1785.

*The Legislative Building
in Fredericton, N.B., was
built in 1880. This
Victorian edifice contains
many artistic treasures.*

The historic Algonquin Hotel, whose turrets dominate the skyline of the town of St. Andrews, N.B., was built in the early 1900s.

The campus of Mount Allison University is one of the loveliest in the east. The first degree given to a woman in the British Empire was awarded by this New Brunswick university in 1875.

The world's largest
covered bridge is found
in Hartland, N.B. Built in
1899, it measures 391
metres and spans the
Saint John River.

A weathered farmhouse
near Wood Point, N.B.,
looks out across the
Cumberland Basin.

Nova Scotia

When Penny and I decided to move our family from Toronto to Nova Scotia, a woman asked her, "But how will you ever keep your mind honed?" It was as though we were settling in Patagonia, rather than a province with eight universities and a history that made Toronto's look bloodless and short. Our decision struck some as perverse, and so far as my career as a writer went, even suicidal. "But I'd like to live near the ocean," I'd explain.

Mac Perry would have understood. A lanky, eloquent magazine editor in Vancouver, he was born in England, but his love of oceans led him to the Pacific for good. After I'd settled in Halifax, he told me in a letter, "There is always a strangely privileged feeling here on this coast when we read about yours. I suppose that a sentimental man, or one deep into the lunatic soup, might now and again think of our nation as being two exquisite extremities with a great wad of something rather less wholesome in between." That's not only a highly original definition of Canada, it's also a neat expression of the special smugness among us who've uprooted our lives in favour of an ocean.

Native Nova Scotians are less self-conscious about the sea. Some have been hearing it since they first drew breath. They grew up knowing in their marrow that, as my father put it, "Something wet and salt/ Creeps and loafs and marches round the continent,/ Careless of time, careless of change, obeying the moon." Still, they do not take the ocean for granted. How could they? It dominates their weather as it dominates their history, and the province is so skinny it's hard to find a spot more than a half-hour's drive from salt water. They go to the sea, and the sea comes to them.

Nova Scotia is only 576 kilometres long, but the shoreline—with fingers of ocean stabbing for miles into the rock, trees, farmland and towns—is longer than the breadth of Canada. It winds along 7579 kilometres of beaches like white satin, coves like secret stone bowls, headlands drenched in furious surf, and in Cape Breton, cliffs that give every sensible sailor the shudders.

For a sense of the sea's power, however, Peggy's Cove is matchless. It's close to Halifax, and one of the most photographed fishing villages in the world. In summer, visitors pile off the tour buses, and swarm like ants across its strange plains of granite. Every so often, the ocean plucks some poor devil off the stone and pulverizes him, and Peggy's Cove is not a place where you'd expect to find people on a violent winter Sunday. But you do. Couples struggle over the granite on foot, and with the February wind lashing their faces, gaze at the terrible, swaying sea. They huddle in the lee of the famous lighthouse and then, with their cheeks red and their eyes bright, report to the restaurant on the rocks. Steaming bowls of lobster-and-haddock chowder never tasted better. I've been out there on just such an afternoon, and found the restaurant jammed with chatty people who had not been able to resist the lure of the sea.

"Ay, the lure of it," Thomas Raddall wrote. Nova Scotia's finest historical novelist, he writes most movingly when he describes the sea. "The sleek and flexuous body of it that's like the swell of breast and hip in the only woman you ever really loved," he continued. And, "the sea wind that made the shingles fly, that brought the parson's chimney down, that shook all the fish-houses and whistled about the wharves, that gathered the spume in fat yellow balls and bowled them over the shoreside roads as you'd blow the froth off your beer."

Shingles, fish-houses, chimneys, wharves, and roads are all man-made. They remind me of something Nova Scotia's coast has that British Columbia's hasn't: the smell of history. When I took Vancouver novelist L.R. (Bunny) Wright for her first drive along a Nova Scotia shore, she marvelled, "Everything looks so *old.*" The west coast also has fish-houses and wharves but, here, there's something about them that convinces you they're merely the latest among centuries of fish-houses and wharves. There's something, too, about the traditional shapes of the houses, and the way they confront the wind down in the coves and up on the seaside hills. The west coast is mild and beautiful, but with respect to European settlement, it is too young to be interesting. You cannot walk among the gulls of a port like Lunenburg without realizing that Nova Scotia is a true marriage of the sea to the ancient story of human struggle.

Nova Scotia, of course, has no monopoly on sea-going history, ocean-driven weather, roaring tides, or wildly varying coastal scenery, but somehow, here in bluenose country, they combine to lend endearing drama to the changing lives of those who have chosen to stay here. Out of the drama, I sometimes think, I may yet achieve some sort of wisdom.

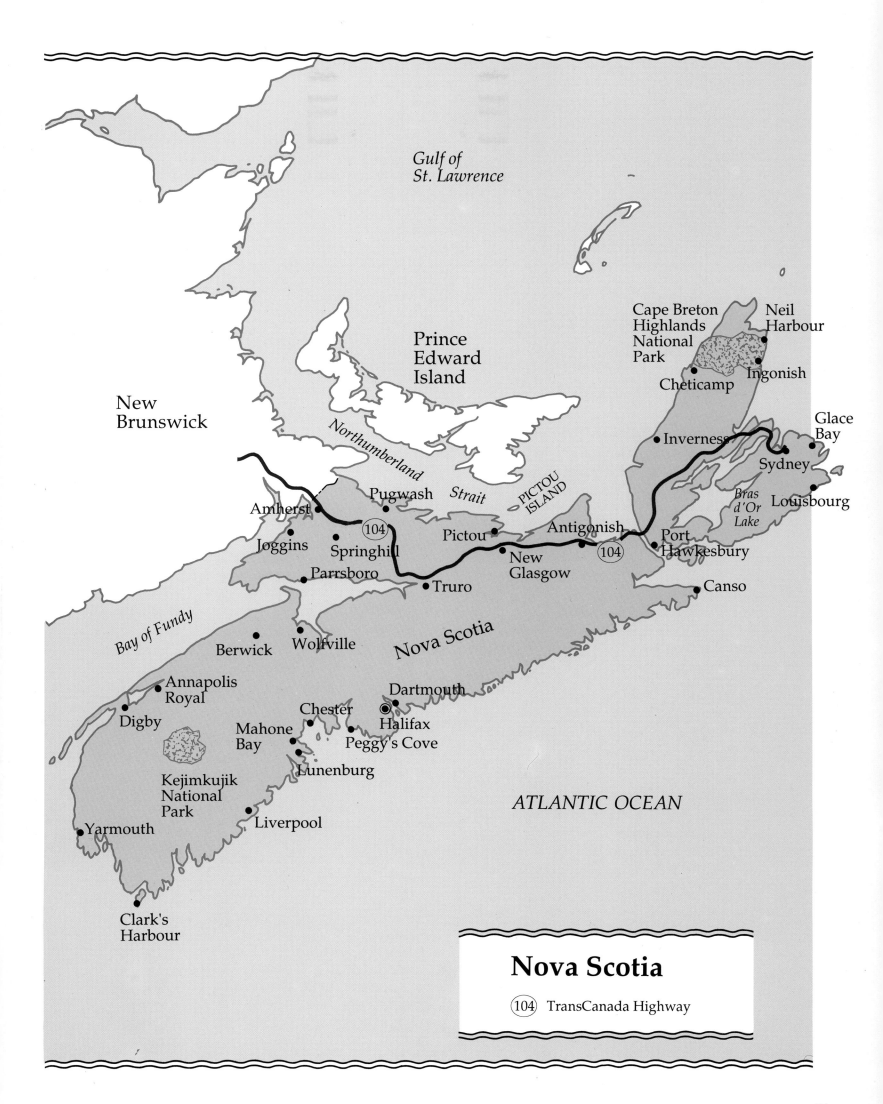

Gulf of
St. Lawrence

Cape Breton
Highlands
National
Park

Neil
Harbour

Prince
Edward
Island

Cheticamp

Ingonish

New
Brunswick

Glace
Bay

Inverness

Sydney

Northumberland

Louisbourg

Pugwash

*Bras
d'Or
Lake*

Strait

PICTOU
ISLAND

Amherst

Antigonish

Pictou

104

Port
Hawkesbury

Joggins

104

Springhill

New
Glasgow

Parrsboro

Canso

Truro

Bay of Fundy

Nova Scotia

Berwick

Wolfville

Annapolis
Royal

Dartmouth

Digby

Chester

Mahone
Bay

Halifax

Peggy's Cove

Lunenburg

ATLANTIC OCEAN

Kejimkujik
National
Park

Yarmouth

Liverpool

Clark's
Harbour

Nova Scotia

104 TransCanada Highway

Nova Scotia

Tourism Bureau
Box 130
Halifax, N.S.
B3J 2M7
Tel.: 1-800-565-0000

Area: 55 491 square km
Length of coastline: 7579 km
Capital: Halifax
Population: 874,000
Flower: Mayflower

Halifax and the Lighthouse Route

The largest city in the Atlantic provinces and the capital of Nova Scotia, Halifax is a fascinating blend of the historic and modern. Restored 18th-century wooden and stone structures mix successfully with contemporary buildings. One of the best examples of this mixture is the waterfront area. Historic Properties is a collection of 12 buildings, several dating back to the early 1800s, which now houses stores and specialty shops. During the summer, town criers, buskers, and visitors mingle on the cobblestones. Harbour tours and boat trips are offered day and night, including sailings aboard the *Bluenose II*, which was built in 1963 in Lunenburg as a replica of the original *Bluenose* (1921-46). And yet, just blocks away, Scotia Square and the city's central business district provide all the modern conveniences one could wish for.

Overlooking Halifax and its harbour is the Citadel National Historic Park, the premier historic attraction for visitors to the city. The fortress was built in 1828-56, and at present offers an Army Museum, a 50-minute sight-and-sound presentation on Halifax and its harbour, a gift shop, and a period food service. At the foot of Citadel Hill and across from the Metro Centre is the Old Town Clock, one of Halifax's best-known landmarks. The timepiece was completed in 1803 and served as the garrison clock.

The Public Gardens on Spring Garden Road are one of the oldest formal Victorian gardens in North America. Established in 1867, the site includes a duck pond, lawns, fountains, and benches.

At the south end of Young Avenue, Point Pleasant Park looks out on the harbour and provides a quiet haven for pedestrians. The Prince of Wales Martello Tower, built during the 1790s, is one of several fortifications that can be visited within the park.

Dalhousie University, founded in 1818, is a non-denominational institution with a student population of 9,000. The faculties of law and medicine are world-renowned. The Dalhousie Art Gallery features Canadian drawings and Canadian, American, and European paintings, sculpture, prints, archaeology, and graphics.

The South Shore, extending from Halifax to the western point of Nova Scotia, is known as the Lighthouse Route. It is filled with picturesque villages such as Peggy's Cove, one of Canada's most photographed and painted spots. This quintessential fishing village consists of a lighthouse perched high up on huge, wave-washed granite boulders, colourful houses, weathered wharves, and fishing boats.

The scenic summer resort of Chester is situated on a peninsula at the head of Mahone Bay. First settled by New England families in 1760, several buildings in the town date from the early 1800s. Across Mahone Bay is Oak Island, where people still seek the treasure which Captain Kidd is thought to have buried there.

Renowned for its shipbuilding and as the home of the *Bluenose* schooners, Lunenburg is built on a peninsula with a front and back harbour. This situation made the port an ideal base for fishing the Grand Banks. A visit to the Fisheries Museum of the Atlantic brings history vividly to life.

The Loyalist Town of Shelburne was first settled in 1783 when approximately 3,000 United Empire Loyalists arrived in 30 ships from New York City. Over the next few years the population of the town grew to 16,000, making it one of the largest communities in North America. After 1787 the population quickly declined and the remaining residents built Shelburne into a fishing and shipbuilding centre. Many of Shelburne's houses date to the Loyalist period, and several of them currently serve as museums.

The most southerly point of Nova Scotia is Cape Sable Island, where submerged ledges extending a long way into the sea and powerful tides have caused hundreds of ships to be lost. It is also the home of the famous Cape Island boat, first built in 1907 in Clark's Harbour. Today the design is a standard for small boats that require high stability and efficiency in the North Atlantic.

Yarmouth and the French Shore

Yarmouth is the province's largest seaport west of Halifax, and is full of souvenirs of the great days of sail. Many of these are exhibited at the Yarmouth County Museum. Also on display is the Runic Stone, a huge stone with inscriptions that some experts believe were carved by Norsemen about 1000 years ago. The historic Yarmouth light, near Yarmouth harbour, was built in 1840. Yarmouth has a daily ferry schedule to Portland and Bar Harbour, Maine.

The villages along the French shore (east along the Bay of Fundy from Yarmouth) were first settled in 1768 by Acadians who had been expelled from Nova Scotia by the English in 1755. Every summer there are Acadian festivals celebrating this heritage, such as the one at Church Point (Pointe de l'Eglise). This village is host to the oldest Acadian festival in the province, Festival Acadien de Clare, held every year during the second week of July in conjunction with celebrations in other Acadian villages along the shore. Church Point is dominated by St. Mary's, the tallest and largest wooden church in North America. Constructed between 1903 and 1905, the spire of the church reaches 56.3 metres.

The largest urban centre in the area, Digby is also an important shipping point. A ferry makes three trips daily between Digby and Saint John, N.B. It is also possible to arrange to go deep-sea fishing or whale-watching. One of the largest scallop fleets in the world is based in Digby; every August the town celebrates Scallop Days in honour of its major industry.

Proceeding west on Digby Neck, a long finger of land pointing out into the Bay of Fundy, one comes first to Long Island, and then Briar Island, both accessible by ferry. Briar Island was the boyhood home of Captain Joshua Slocum, who gained fame as the first man to sail alone around the world. He made the voyage between 1895 and 1898 in a 12-metre sloop. A memorial plaque to Captain Slocum is found at the southern end of the island. The area is also good for bird- and whale-watching.

The historic town of Annapolis Royal was founded in 1605, making it the oldest settlement in Canada. Called Port Royal by the French, it was originally situated 8 km down the Annapolis River, where the Port Royal National Historic Park is now located. The town, which was once a strong military base, a provincial capital, and a shipping and commercial centre, is dotted with buildings of considerable historical significance, such as the O'Dell Inn Museum (circa 1869), the Robertson-McNamara House (circa 1785), and the Adams-Ritchie House (1712). The Annapolis Royal Historic Gardens have approximately 2 km of pathways, accessible to wheelchairs, which wind through gardens of outstanding beauty. Fort Anne National Historic Park represents one of the most fought-over places in Canada. Belonging alternately to the French and then to the English, it was the scene of over 15 sieges and raids.

The Port Royal National Historic Park is a 10.5-km drive from Annapolis Royal. The Port Royal Habitation was the earliest European settlement in North America north of Florida, established by De Mons and Champlain in 1605. It is here that North America's first play was written and produced - Marc Lescarbot's *Le Théâtre de Neptune* in 1606.

Glooscap Trail

Named after the hero of Micmac legend, this tourist trail makes its way around the Minas Basin, from Cape Blomidon to Amherst near the New Brunswick border. The area around Wolfville, especially the village of Grand Pré, is important in Acadian history. Grand Pré is the site of one of the earliest French settlements in the province, and was the setting for Longfellow's poem *Evangeline.* In Grand Pré National Historic Park a stone church of French design stands as a memorial to Acadian culture and houses a number of historical displays about the Acadians. Outside the church is a statue of Longfellow's Evangeline. One aspect of the later history of the village is signalled by the presence of the Covenanters Church, which was built by Loyalists in 1804. It is found on a hill near the park.

Wolfville is a charming university town which was settled in the 1760s by New England Planters. Acadia University occupies the centre of town. The Acadia University Gallery in the Beveridge Arts Centre houses many works by the internationally-acclaimed artist Alex Colville, who lives in the town.

Known as the "Hub of Nova Scotia," Truro has been a major railroad town since 1858, and is now on the main line of the Canadian National Railway between Montreal and Halifax. Historical attractions include the Colchester Historical Society Museum and the Little White School House Museum. In Victoria Park hiking, tennis, picnic grounds and a scenic view of two waterfalls are available.

The town of Parrsboro is used as a headquarters by rock hounds who come to Minas Basin looking for semi-precious stones, such as agate and amethyst, that are found on the beaches and in the cliffs. In 1985, geologists working near Parrsboro discovered the largest cache of fossilized bones ever found in North America. Included in this find were very rare shells and jaws of the reptiles most closely related to mammals.

Nearby Joggins is famous for its Coal Age rock formations in which fossilized trees and other plants can be seen in the 50-metre sandstone cliffs. Many of the fossil trees were half-buried while still alive and can now be seen standing upright as they grew.

Along the Northumberland Strait

The Scottish heritage of Nova Scotia is apparent in this section of the province. Pugwash is the site of the annual July 1 Gathering of the Clans, and this community has street signs in English and Gaelic. In Pictou, a statue of a bonneted and kilted Scot stands as a monument to colonists who came from Scotland in the bark *Hector* in 1773. On a beach near Lismore is a cairn in memory of Angus MacDonald, Hugh MacDonald, and John MacPherson - "soldiers of Prince Charlie" - who were among the Scots defeated by the English at Culloden in 1746. Antigonish is the home of Canada's oldest Highland games, held each July since 1861. Scots from all over gather for the best in Scottish music, dance, and sports.

Cape Breton

Some of the most spectacular scenery and fascinating history in Nova Scotia are found on the island of Cape Breton. Scottish settlers

remembered their homeland when settling in Cape Breton, and towns and villages such as Dundee, Inverness, Iona, and Dunvegan show this heritage. The influence of the native Micmac Indians is strong around Bras d'Or Lake, with reserves such as Eskasoni, Wagmatcook, and Whycocomagh lining its shores. At Whycocomagh native craftsmen sell their basketry, wood carving, and silk-screen prints at four local handicraft shops. The Acadians also settled in Cape Breton, in such areas as Isle Madame in the south and Chéticamp in the Cape Breton Highlands. Les Trois Pignons serves the Chéticamp community as the centre of Acadian French heritage.

Fortress of Louisbourg National Historic Park includes the largest historical reconstruction project in Canada. One-quarter of the 18th-century town has been restored, including some 50 buildings and extensive stone fortifications. The Fortress of Louisbourg Museum displays plans and drawings of the original fort and accounts of the various sieges of its history.

More recent history comes alive at two sites in Cape Breton. At the Alexander Graham Bell National Historic Park in Baddeck, a museum displays replicas of early telephone equipment and examples of Bell's lesser-known inventions. And a new National Historic Site exhibit at Table Head in Glace Bay honours Guglielmo Marconi's role in the development of modern global communications. Marconi established a wireless telegraph station at Table Head in 1902, from which he transmitted the first transatlantic wireless message from North America to England.

The Cabot Trail is one of the most beautiful drives in North America. This highway around the northern part of Cape Breton Island curves around sea-swept headlands, skirts the edge of sheer cliffs, and contains many lookout points. The trail was named after John Cabot, the great navigator and explorer who first sighted Cape Breton island on June 23, 1497.

More than one-third of the Cabot Trail is in Cape Breton Highland's National Park. The park is approximately 958 square km in area, borders both the Gulf of St. Lawrence and the Atlantic Ocean, and forms part of a great tableland which in many places rises precipitously from sea level to a height of 538 metres. It is the largest remaining wilderness in the province.

*The Barachois River
winds down through the
Cape Breton Highlands
of Nova Scotia.*

The shifting sands of Sable Island have begun to engulf this abandoned house. Located more than 300 km east of Halifax, N.S., this strip of sand is known as the "graveyard of the Atlantic," having caused over 200 shipwrecks. The island is also home to approximately 200 wild horses.

*Encircled by mountains,
the village of Red River,
N.S. lies slightly north of
Cape Breton Highlands
National Park.*

The Public Gardens in Halifax, N.S., are one of the oldest formal Victorian gardens in North America. Established in 1867, the site includes a duck pond, lawns, fountains, and benches.

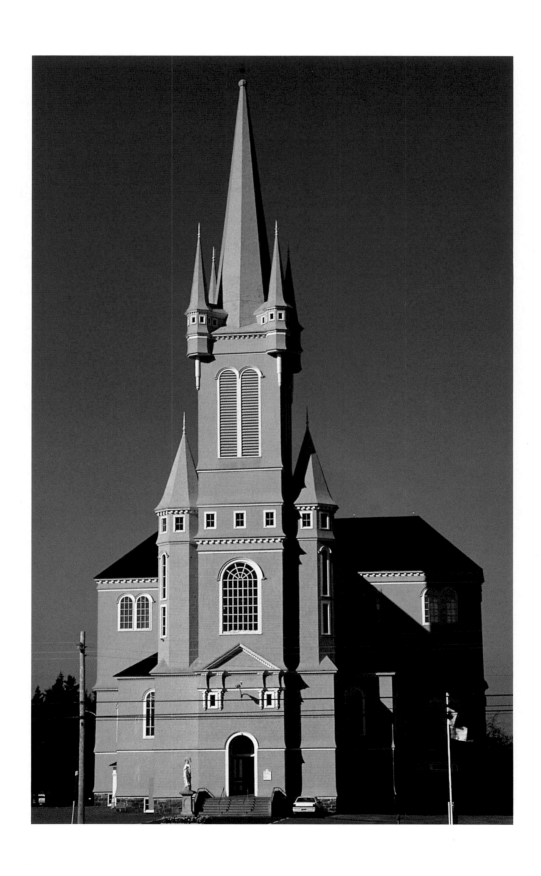

The historic town of Annapolis Royal was founded in 1605, making it the oldest settlement in Canada. Fort Anne National Historic Park features several buildings which date back centuries, including this British Officers' Quarters, built in 1797.

Previous pages:

Middle Head is the site of the Keltic Lodge, a province-run resort hotel within Cape Breton Highlands National Park. The lodge's site commands a beautiful view of the Ingonish coastline and the surrounding highlands.

Many of the houses in Shelburne, N.S., date to the Loyalist period of the town. The community was first settled in 1783 when approximately 3,000 United Empire Loyalists arrived in 30 ships from New York City.

The Annapolis Valley in Nova Scotia is well-known for its fruit farms which harvest apples, pears, plums, and strawberries.

*Colourful boats enliven
the landing stage at the
Neil Harbour wharf, on
Cape Breton Island, N.S.*

The Parrsboro Golf Club, in Parrsboro, N.S., is backed by the Cobequid Mountains, and provides a lovely view of rocky inlets and the Minas Basin. The beaches in this area are well-known for their fossils and semi-precious stones.

Located on a ledge high above the point where the Bay of Fundy runs into the Minas Channel in Nova Scotia, the Cape d'Or lighthouse provides a splendid view of shifting tides.

Antigonish is the home of Canada's oldest Highland games, held each July since 1861. Scots from all over gather for the best in Scottish music, dance, and sports.

The town of Pugwash is the site of the annual July 1 Gathering of the Clans. This community displays its Scottish heritage even in its street signs, which are in both English and Gaelic.

This Meeting House was built in Barrington, N.S., in 1765, and was used by early settlers for public meetings and as a place of worship. It is now a museum.

During the summer, town criers, buskers, and visitors mingle on the cobblestones of Historic Properties in Halifax, N.S. This restoration project houses stores and specialty shops.

Various styles of boats are anchored on the waterfront in Halifax.

Renowned for its shipbuilding and as the home of the Bluenose schooners, Lunenburg is built on a peninsula with a front and back harbour.

Prince Edward Island

If you're bound for Prince Edward Island for the first time, don't fly. Take a ferry. You'll understand the place better, and grasp why its people sometimes feel that sea and winter hold them hostage. What separates the Island from the mainland is the Northumberland Strait, which can be either a killer or as benign as a mud bath. It depends on the weather.

More than two hundred kilometres long, and at its narrowest, fourteen wide, the strait was already a challenge to mail-carriers more than two centuries ago. From the time of the American Revolution right down to the First World War, teams of men used reinforced skiffs, modified canoes, and glorified dories in scheduled charges over the booby traps of ice and paralyzingly cold water that lay between them and the far shore. Some lost fingers and feet, others their lives.

Even after the federal government's steam-driven ferries arrived on the strait, iceboat crews were pressed into service; ice fields often manacled the steamers and dragged them around offshore, or locked them up in port. The ferries are more powerful and reliable now, and ice-breakers clear the way, but even so, winds and whiteouts are so vicious some days that no vessel dares venture onto the strait. It's at times like these that Islanders most resent the strait's Jekyll-and-Hyde character, and also what they see as Canada's failure to keep an old promise. When the Island joined Confederation 117 years ago, Canada was to provide "efficient steam service for the conveyance of mails and passengers ... between the Island and the mainland ... Winter and Summer."

I was eighteen when I first crossed the strait. On my way to play college basketball in Charlottetown, I sailed on the pride of the government fleet, the *Abegweit*. (The ancient Micmac word for the Island, *Abegweit*, meant either "afloat on the waves close by," or "moored in the shelter of the encircling shore.") Compared to the dinky ferryboats of my boyhood, which floated on Toronto Harbour like wind-driven hats, the 112-metre *Abegweit* struck me as an ocean liner. I later learned she had eight sets of diesel engines, and four big nickel propellers, but out on the strait in the winter of 1953, all I knew was that I loved her oily odour and steady shudder, her ability to barge through the ice and make cracks in it that zigzagged far ahead, and the way the seagulls hovered so close to her decks I could see the texture of their feet and feathers.

The *Abegweit*'s speed was 16.5 knots, and pretty soon, I could make out patches of the Island's famous red soil in the low, snowy bluffs of the south coast. Returning from Saskatchewan in 1891, a desperately homesick Island teenager crossed these same waters, and told her diary, "I kept an eager look-out for land and the minute I saw it I flew like the wind to get a good look at the 'ould sod.'" She was Lucy Maud Montgomery, and one day she'd write *Anne of Green Gables.*

Thanks to that tricky barrier, the strait, Islanders have managed to preserve some of the flavour of Montgomery's "ould sod." Granted, the automobile, which they reviled long after it had become a love object on the mainland, has irrevocably changed the Island. So have any number of 20th-century inventions and forces. But from the highest hills—and none is higher than 150 metres—you can still look around in mid-summer and understand why Islanders of Montgomery's time proudly dubbed their province "the Garden of the Gulf."

Farm fields still look like undulating, patchwork quilts of pale green, brick red, Irish green, and chocolate brown. Hilltop firs still stand dark against the sky. Villages may shrink, shopping malls sprout, and fast-food joints creep across the land, just as they do in other places. But on the Island, brooks still gurgle among ferns in woodsy dells, great combers still crash and roll on deserted beaches, and starlight still glitters on black tidal ponds. Montgomery would be pleased to know that, even now, the Island boasts farmhouses in which a little girl, just before drifting off to sleep, might hear the whispered conversations of trees with souls.

Like their forebears, many Islanders are crazy about harness-racing, and one morning in late November, I found myself at the Charlottetown Driving Park with nothing to do. Sunlight and warmth lingered in the fresh, damp, moving air, and the grass was unseasonably green. Nine horses pulling sulkies nipped around the track. They were getting their morning trot, their constitutional. The ones on the inside ran clockwise, the ones on the outside counterclockwise, and they were all pretty, sprightly, head-tossing beasties.

Clip, clop. Snort, snort.

The middle-aged drivers looked as smug as boys who had just learned their school had closed indefinitely for repairs. I sat down in the stands by myself, poured a cup of steaming coffee from my thermos, lit up a cigarette, and enjoyed this quintessentially Island scene for a full half-hour. Change, I knew, must always come marching over the strait from the mainland, but I hoped its invasion in future would be graceful, gentle, and above all, slow. I liked the Island just as it was.

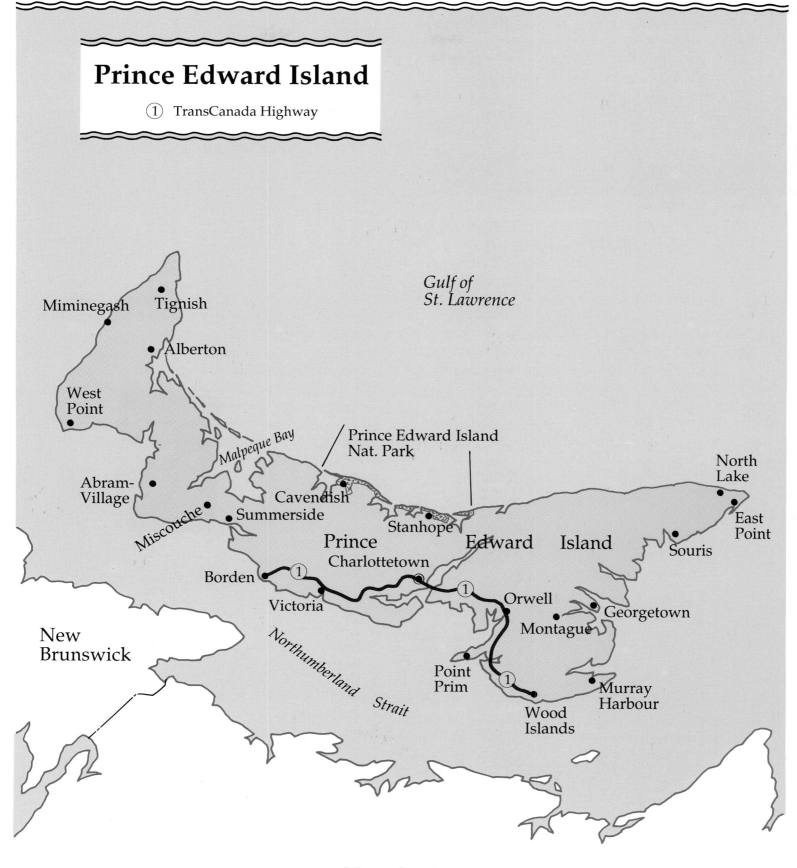

Prince Edward Island

① TransCanada Highway

Gulf of St. Lawrence

Miminegash

Tignish

Alberton

West Point

Abram-Village

Malpeque Bay

Prince Edward Island Nat. Park

North Lake

East Point

Cavendish

Miscouche

Summerside

Stanhope

Souris

Prince

Edward

Island

Charlottetown

Borden

Victoria

Orwell

Georgetown

Montague

New Brunswick

Northumberland Strait

Point Prim

Wood Islands

Murray Harbour

Nova Scotia

Prince Edward Island

Dept. of Tourism and Parks
Box 940, Dept. 8
Charlottetown, P.E.I.
C1A 7M5
1-800-565-0267

Area: 5 657 square km
Length of coastline: 1260 km
Capital: Charlottetown
Population: 128,000
Flower: Lady's slipper

Charlottetown and Central Prince Edward Island

Called the Cradle of Confederation, Charlottetown is the smallest provincial capital in Canada. The only city in Prince Edward Island, Charlottetown's peaceful streets are lined with stately churches, historic buildings and Victorian houses. A mixture of government, university, and tourist town, Charlottetown is also known for entertainment. The Confederation Centre of the Arts, which was built in 1964 as a national memorial to the Fathers of Confederation, includes an art gallery and museum, a provincial library, memorial hall, restaurant, and two theatres. Each summer the Charlottetown Festival mounts an entertaining season which invariably includes the popular musical adaptation of *Anne of Green Gables.*

Opposite Confederation Centre is Province House, where the articles that led to the union of all the British North American colonies into a united Canada were signed in 1867. Other notable buildings in Charlottetown include Government House, home of Prince Edward Island's lieutenant governor, and Beaconsfield, headquarters of the Prince Edward Island Museum and Heritage Foundation. St. Dunstan's Basilica, situated south of Province House, is one of Canada's largest churches. It is known for its twin Gothic spires, impressive altar, and fine Italian carvings.

Prince Edward Island National Park stretches for about 40 km along the north shore of the island, along the Gulf of St. Lawrence. Some of the finest white sand beaches in eastern Canada are found here, as well as sand dunes, red sandstone cliffs, salt marshes, and freshwater pools. The best-known beaches are Brackley, Cavendish, Rustico, and Stanhope. Camp sites, supervised swimming beaches, and a golf course are popular features of the park.

The northern part of Central Prince Edward Island is *Anne of Green Gables* country. Cavendish is a mecca for fans of Lucy Maud Montgomery's many novels. The famous house which was used by the author as Anne's home in the novel is now a museum in Prince Edward Island National Park. Other settings in the book, such as Lovers' Lane, the Haunted Woods, and Anne's Babbling Brook are nearby. Miss Montgomery's grave can be found in the Cavendish cemetery. Serious fans will want to visit her birthplace in New London, and perhaps even travel 10 km north to Park Corner, where the Anne of Green Gables Museum is located.

Historic Malpeque was first settled by the French in the early 1700s; before this it was the site of a Micmac encampment. Many Scots settled there in 1770. The flower gardens at Malpeque feature 400 colours and varieties of dahlia, rose gardens, sunken gardens, and other attractions.

The first stop for most visitors to Prince Edward Island is Borden, where the ferry terminal is situated. Ferries cross the Northumberland Strait between Borden and Cape Tormentine, N.B., a distance of 14 km.

East along the Northumberland Strait, the small community of Victoria-by-the-Sea is a scenic stop. There is an active summer-stock theatre based in the community hall.

Directly across the harbour from Charlottetown is Rocky Point, where there are two interesting historic sites. Fort Amherst/Port La Joye National Historic Park consists of earthworks where Port La Joye, the first permanent European settlement on the Island, had been established by the French in 1720. When the British later captured the settlement in 1758, they built Fort Amherst, a series of defences which later fell into disrepair. Nearby, the Micmac Indian Village reconstructs the life of the Micmac Indian on Prince Edward Island before the arrival of the Europeans. Tableaux include birch-bark wigwams, a council place,

a smoke house and a sweat house. The museum at the site features actual tools and weapons used by these first inhabitants of the Island.

West Coast

Summerside is the Island's second-largest community, and the principal port for potato shipments. The annual Summerside Lobster Carnival in mid-July draws people from all over the region. They come for the lobster suppers, harness-racing, fiddling, and step-dancing contests.

The Acadian Museum in Miscouche is a good introduction to the Evangeline Region, which extends west along Bedeque Bay and Egmont Bay. At Mont Carmel the Acadian Pioneer Village recreates an early (1800-1820) Acadian Pioneer settlement. And at Abram-Village, Le Festival Acadien is held every Labour Day weekend in conjunction with the annual Egmont Bay and Mont-Carmel Agricultural Exhibition. Acadian handcrafts, livestock, and farm produce are displayed.

At Alberton it is possible to charter a boat in order to go deep-sea fishing. Nearby are the Kildare Capes, red sandstone cliffs which have been carved by the tides over the last thousand years. This is the spot where Jacques Cartier is traditionally thought to have first sighted Prince Edward Island, before proceeding to the northwestern-most tip of the Island, Cape North. There is an international laboratory for testing and evaluating wind generators located at Cape North.

East Coast

There are many historical attractions on the east coast of Prince Edward Island. At Orwell Corner Historic Village, on the southern route from Charlottetown, crops and livestock are raised and tended as they were in the late 1800s. The buildings, dating from 1864 to 1896, include a combined store, post office, and farmhouse, as well as barns, a school, and a church. The summer programme includes musical evenings.

At Point Prim, the oldest lighthouse on the Island (1846), is still in use. This tower is the only round, brick structure in Canada.

Continuing east, one comes to Murray Head peninsula. At Murray Harbour there is a Log Cabin Museum which houses antiques. And another of Prince Edward Island's fine white sand beaches is found at Panmore Island. It features sand dunes which are up to six metres high.

Northeastern Prince Edward Island is popular with sport fishermen from around the world. Many come to North Lake each year to fish for the giant bluefin tuna. For those interested in the history of commercial fishing in Prince Edward Island, the Basin Head Fisheries Museum displays photographs and marine equipment.

*A winter sunset reflects
off water and ice near
Cape Tryon, P.E.I.*

Previous pages:
*Red sandstone cliffs,
such as these found
near Cavendish beach,
are a distinctive feature
of Prince Edward Island.*

A meadow of wildflowers stretches down to the sea in eastern Prince Edward Island.

*A separate bell tower is
an original feature of
this church at
Springbrook, P.E.I.*

Made famous by the novels of Lucy Maud Montgomery, Green Gables is now a museum in P.E.I. National Park. Near the house are other settings from Anne of Green Gables, such as Lovers' Lane, the Haunted Woods and Anne's Babbling Brook.

*A group of Charlottetown
notables enjoys a
reception at Government
House, home of P.E.I.'s
lieutenant governor.*

A crowd gathers for the Blessing of the Fleet in the Evangeline Region of P.E.I. The majority of the Island's Acadian settlements is found along this southwest stretch.

Vivid colours adorn the outbuildings of a dairy farm near New Glasgow, P.E.I.

Following pages:
A red gate accents the green fields of a farm in central Prince Edward Island.

89

Called "the cradle of Confederation," Charlottetown, P.E.I., is the smallest provincial capital in Canada. Its pleasant streets are lined with stately churches, historic buildings, and Victorian houses.

Newfoundland

The lighthouse at Cape St. Mary's, Nfld., is dwarfed by the dramatic cliffs of the western shore of the Avalon Peninsula.

I was forty when I first saw Newfoundland, and it struck me as a quirky country with odd beer labels. But it's not a country, you say, it's a *province*. Well maybe, but when Newfoundlanders talk about going out to the west coast they don't mean Vancouver, they mean Corner Brook, or Bonne Bay, and when I began a speech in St. John's by saying how happy I was to be in "your country," the crowd cheered. Moreover, the beer labels seemed to be a declaration of independence.

When Newfoundland joined Canada in 1949, the deal guaranteed the survival of local trademarks. Thus it was that, when the Labatt's interests of Ontario bought out Bavarian Brewing of Newfoundland, they maintained Bavarian's "Black Label" ale. This meant that, although Black Label was Carling's Black Label to all other Canadians, it was Labatt's Black Label to Newfoundlanders. For similar reasons, India Pale Ale was Labatt's I.P.A. to millions of Canadian guzzlers, but among Newfoundlanders, it was Molson's I.P.A. Moreover, Black Horse Ale had vanished across the country (across Canada, that is), but it thrived in Newfoundland.

It was in Newfoundland that I heard the most blatant exploitation of local patriotism in the history of TV beer commercials. It showed a bunch of worthies in a tavern, drinking Blue Star. The chorus ended with a rousing toast, and went like this:

Blue Star, Blue Star
The finest in the land,
You can drink a toast to Newfoundland
With a Blue Star in your hand

And then, all together now, and beer on high:

Up she comes!

Newfoundland always delivers what I want out of travel: amiable times with a distinctive people in a dramatic land. The capital, St. John's, boasts only about 85,000 residents, but dark, stupendous cliffs define the harbour bowl, and for centuries the city has been living right out there among the greatest fishing grounds, the greatest storms and icebergs, and the greatest ships in the history of the world. It has always been a haven for seafarers, and remains the most cosmopolitan small city in all of English-speaking Canada. For a mainlander with a local acquaintance or two, St. John's is a city in which loneliness is impossible. As writer Jan Morris wrote in *Saturday Night*, it's "windy, fishy, anecdotal, proud, weather-beaten, quirky, obliging, ornery, and fun." And very Irish. Up she comes!

But St. John's is still only St. John's. To see a bit of outport Newfoundland - all coastal settlements, other than the capital, are outports - I once boarded a government supply ship at Lewisporte ("The Gateway to the North") for a milk run to Labrador. The ship was the *Petite Forte*, and on a warm, rosy July evening, she glided out on Burnt Bay, chugged between Job's Cove and Comfort Island, and headed north.

The voyage was especially happy. Wives of crew and their excited children were aboard for this particular trip, and before dark, girls of thirteen and fourteen huddled above the bridge, and with their faces pointing north and their hair streaming south, sang good songs. The stars came out, the northern lights cavorted dead ahead, the *Petite Forte*'s searchlights explored the ice cakes that speckled her radar screen, and the smell off the evergreen shore and the inky ocean was impossibly clean.

We were bound for Nippers Harbour, Fishot Islands, Paradise River—twenty-two outports in all—and by the time the vessel had reached Goose Bay, Labrador, turned around, and visited them all over again, she'd have spent ten days steaming more than 1,550 nautical miles. She moved steadily north with matter-of-fact relentlessness. To outports that had been icebound all winter, she brought everything from bathtubs to Brazilian chocolates, from dental plaster to cement mixers, from stereo sets to macaroni.

I remember how she ducked into each cove, how each pier swarmed with grinning parents, noisy kids, and giddy dogs, how the jokes flew between crew and villagers, and the speed with which the *Petite Forte* unloaded the right cargo, and went about her business. She soon popped back out to the ocean, and trundled onward, ever onward, past a cold wall of towering cliffs, a looming, menacing mess of green and dun rock. Then she disappeared in the wall again. She slipped into another barren cove, where people had somehow been surviving for generations, and an hour later, out she came once more. Her bow turned north.

She crossed the Strait of Belle Isle, which separates the northern tip of the island of Newfoundland from Labrador, on the night of July 9. In a Newfoundland parallel to the ceremonies aboard ocean liners crossing the equator, the crew donned rubber boots and slickers, and with their faces swathed in white cloth, chased the children. The crew claimed to be King Neptune and his henchmen. Laughing and squealing, the youngsters ran from stem to stern, but Neptune's gang got them all, and smeared their faces with chocolate syrup.

The game reminded me that it's not so much the brutal majesty of the coastline that I like about Newfoundland. It's the people. It's their kindness, humour, pride, and even after centuries of hardship, their undying ability to enjoy being with one another. I like them, too, for their cultural confidence. They know who they are. You don't hear much about an "identity crisis" over there.

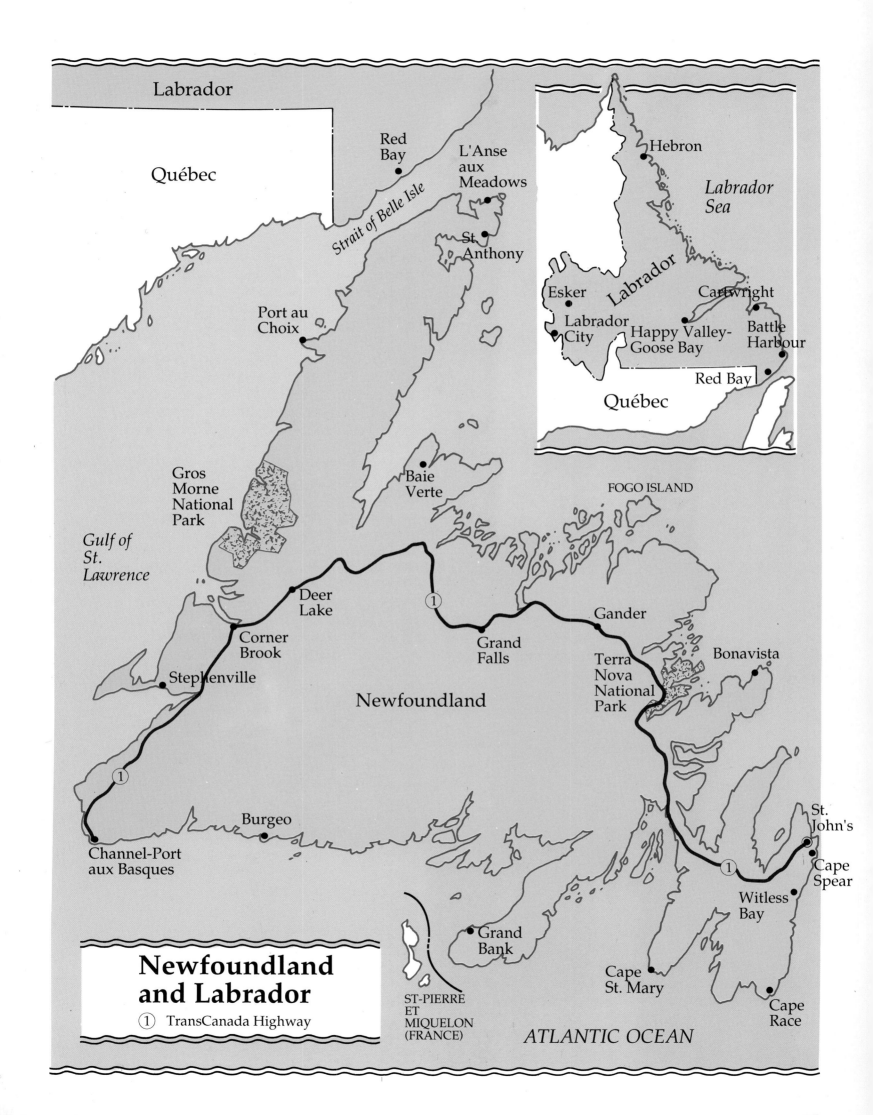

Labrador

Québec

Red
Bay

L'Anse
aux
Meadows

Strait of Belle Isle

St.
Anthony

Port au
Choix

Gros
Morne
National
Park

*Gulf of
St.
Lawrence*

Deer
Lake

Corner
Brook

Stephenville

Newfoundland

Baie
Verte

FOGO ISLAND

① Grand
Falls

Gander

Terra
Nova
National
Park

Bonavista

St.
John's

Cape
Spear

Witless
Bay

Burgeo

Channel-Port
aux Basques

ST-PIERRE
ET
MIQUELON
(FRANCE)

Grand
Bank

Cape
St. Mary

Cape
Race

ATLANTIC OCEAN

Hebron

*Labrador
Sea*

Esker

Cartwright

Labrador
City

Happy Valley-
Goose Bay

Battle
Harbour

Red Bay

Québec

Newfoundland
and Labrador

① TransCanada Highway

97

Newfoundland

Dept. of Development and Tourism
Box 2016
St. John's, Newfoundland
A1C 5R8
1-800-563-6353

Area: 404 517 square km
Length of coastline: 28 957 km
Capital: St. John's
Population: 568,349
Flower: Pitcher plant

St. John's and the Avalon Peninsula

One of the oldest settlements in North America and the capital city of Newfoundland and Labrador, St. John's has a long and varied history. Its name dates back to John Cabot's discovery of Newfoundland on June 24, 1497, the feast day of St. John the Baptist. For the next few centuries the French and English fought for possession of the land until the British won a final victory in 1762.

From Signal Hill, one of Canada's oldest and largest National Historic Parks, there is a superb view of the city, its harbour, and the adjacent coastline. In the park it is possible to visit the Queen's Battery, fortifications that date from the Napoleonic Wars, and watch the Signal Hill Tattoo, in which soldiers dressed in period uniform re-enact colonial military exercises. Gibbet Hill, near the Interpretation Centre, was used to display criminals who had been hanged. At the top of Signal Hill stands Cabot Tower. Constructed in 1897, it commemorates the 400th anniversary of Cabot's discovery of Newfoundland and the diamond jubilee of Queen Victoria. An exhibition in the tower tells the story of Guglielmo Marconi - the Italian inventor who received the first trans-Atlantic wireless message there, from Cornwall, England.

Beside Signal Hill lies Quidi Vidi Village, an active fishing village with its own miniature harbour. Because the villagers have refused to be resettled into St. John's, the city has grown to surround them instead. Quidi Vidi looks much the same today as it did a century ago, with trap skiffs moored in front of the fishermen's stores and nets spread to dry on the grass. Nearby Quidi Vidi Lake is the site of the annual St. John's Regatta, held on the first Wednesday of August. This is the oldest continuous sporting event in North America - a day of rowing races on the lake and of food and games in the fairway.

In downtown St. John's, brightly-painted wooden houses line the steep hills which lead to the harbour. Water Street is one of the oldest thoroughfares in North America, having been the centre of commercial activity in the city for over four hundred years. It is lined with a variety of interesting stores, restaurants, and pubs. The nearby Murray Premises is a restored mercantile complex on the harbour front. Here boutiques are mixed with displays that reflect the maritime, military, and natural history of the province. The Newfoundland Museum on Duckworth Street has an excellent collection of artifacts from the native peoples of the province.

The arts are represented at the Resource Centre for the Arts, located in the restored Long Shoreman's Protective Union (LSPU) Hall, as well as at the Arts and Culture Centre. Next to the Arts and Culture Centre is the Memorial University of Newfoundland.

Cape Spear National Historic Park is a short trip from St. John's. The Cape Spear Lighthouse was built in 1835, and is situated on the most easterly point of land in North America. The two-storey, wooden structure is now a museum.

The Avalon Peninsula has several ecological and wilderness reserves. Near Witless Bay three small islands make up the Witless Bay Islands Ecological Reserve. Puffins, petrels, kittiwakes, and Atlantic murres are just some of the birds that nest here. The Avalon Wilderness Area, in the central part of the peninsula, is home to a herd of woodland caribou. Visitors interested in hiking, canoeing, camping, and fishing must obtain a permit from the Department of Tourism in St. John's before entering the area. Cape St. Mary's Ecological Reserve, near St. Bride's

Opposite:
The Atlantic puffin is one of the many birds which nests at the Witless Bay Islands Ecological Reserve on the east coast of the Avalon Peninsula, Nfld.

Brightly-painted wooden houses line the steep hills which lead to the harbour in St. John's, Nfld.

on the western shore of the peninsula, is home to a huge seabird colony. Thousands of gannets nest on Bird Rock, making it the second-largest gannet colony in North America.

The small town of Harbour Grace, overlooking Conception Bay, west of St. John's, played a notable role in the history of modern aviation. It was from here that Wiley Post began a round-the-world flight in 1931, and also from here that Amelia Earhart took off in 1932 on her solo flight to Londonderry, Northern Island.

West Coast

The west coast of Newfoundland is a rugged terrain of seacoasts, forests, and ancient mountains. Ferries from North Sydney, N.S., land at Channel-Port aux Basques. Proceeding north a sign warns drivers about the dangerously strong winds which funnel down from Table Mountain; they have been known to overturn motor vehicles and derail trains.

The town of Stephenville grew in population during the Second World War when the United States government built Harmon Air Force base on the outskirts of the town. The base is now incorporated into the community's industrial park. Every summer the Stephenville Festival features plays ranging from original indigenous works to professional quality productions of Broadway hits.

Directly west of Stephenville is Port au Port Peninsula. The home of the largest French-speaking population in the province, it was once a part of colonial France's fishing territory in Newfoundland. Every summer this heritage is celebrated during Une Longue Veillée, a festival of traditional song, dance, and recitation.

Corner Brook, located at the mouth of the Humber River, is Newfoundland's second-

largest city. A bustling industrial centre with a huge pulp-and-paper mill, the city has many facilities for travellers. The ski centre of Marble Mountain is just outside the city, and nearby Blow Me Down Provincial Park provides a lovely view of the Bay of Islands.

Set in a spectacular portion of the Long Range Mountains, Gros Morne National Park is a region of fjords, mountains, lakes, and ocean vistas, carved centuries ago by glaciers. It was named for Newfoundland's second-highest peak, Gros Morne, which dominates the Bonne Bay area. The area was designated a UNESCO World Heritage Site in 1988. Both natural and human history are well-documented at Visitor's Centres within the park. Camping, hiking, bird-watching, and boating are just some of the recreational activities in which the visitor may participate.

North of Gros Morne are several fascinating historic sites. In Port au Choix National Historic Park a mass of bones, tools, and weapons found in 1967 was identified as belonging to the Maritime Archaic People, a group of hunters and gatherers who lived along the eastern seaboard from Maine to Labrador as early as 2000 B.C. And L'Anse aux Meadows National Historic Park is the site of the only-known Viking settlement in North America. It is believed to be the site of Leif Eiriksson's colony in the New World, dating from around 1000 A.D. A recreation of sod houses lets the visitor experience the life of the period and an Interpretation Centre fills in the details of the history.

Central and Eastern Newfoundland

The town of Grand Falls is the location of one of the saddest chapters in Newfoundland history, the passing of the Beothuk Indians. The Beothuks, a tribe of nomadic hunters and fishermen who lived in central Newfoundland, were exterminated by settlers who hunted them like animals. Mary March, or Demasduit, was one of the two last known Beothuks, and the Mary March Museum in Grand Falls commemorates the tragic demise of her people. The last Beothuk, a girl named Shanawdithit, died at St. John's in 1829.

The islands of Notre Dame Bay are accessible by a series of causeways and car ferry service. Traditional ways of living are still in evidence in these small outports, and Fogo, New World, and Change Island are scenic and interesting stops.

Gander, known as the "Crossroads of the World," is the home of Gander International Airport. In the 1930s it was chosen by the British Air Ministry as the site of a new airbase, and its strategic position was invaluable when the Second World War broke out. It is now the hub of transatlantic commercial airline routes.

Terra Nova National Park is situated on the shore of Bonavista Bay. Numerous lakes and streams, dense, virgin forest, and sheltered bays make this park a popular destination. Both camping facilities and cabins are available.

Cape Bonavista is one of Newfoundland's oldest settlements, and is believed to be the place where John Cabot first landed in 1497. The Cape Bonavista lighthouse was built in 1843 and has now been restored and is open to the public as a Provincial Historic Site and lifestyle museum.

Old Bonaventure is typical of the many tiny outports which are found on the coast of the Bonavista Peninsula, Nfld.

A rusted anchor attests to the Avalon's reputation as the shipwreck peninsula. Thousands of ships sank off the rocky headlands between St. John's, Nfld., and Cape Race.

This stone lighthouse at Rose Blanche Point, was built in 1873. Its design, with the lantern mounted on the roof of the house, is common among older lighthouses in Newfoundland.

Set in a spectacular portion of the Long Range Mountains in western Newfoundland, Gros Morne National Park is a region of fjords, mountains, lakes and ocean vistas, carved centuries ago by glaciers.

Following pages:
The ancient cliffs of Cape Race are often shrouded in mist. The rugged shore of nearby Mistaken Point is the location of the world's richest find of Precambrian fossils.

Situated on the southwest coastal plains region of Newfoundland, Channel-Port aux Basques was a fishing station for the French, Portuguese and Basques as early as the 16th century. Now the community is the principal Marine Atlantic ferry terminal in the province.

Cape St. Mary's Ecological Reserve, near St. Bride's, Nfld., is home to a huge seabird colony. Thousands of gannets nest on Bird Rock, making it the second-largest gannet colony in North America.

L'Anse aux Meadows National Historic Park is the site of the only known Viking settlement in North America. This northern Newfoundland site is believed to date back to 1000 A.D.

From Signal Hill, one of Canada's oldest and largest national historic parks, there is a spectacular view of St. John's, its harbour, and the adjacent coastline. Pictured here are the remains of Fort Amherst.

*The annual St. John's
Regatta is run on the
first Wednesday of
August on Quidi Vidi
Lake. It is considered to
be the oldest organized
sporting event in North
America.*

Built in 1835, the Cape Spear Lighthouse marks the most easterly point in North America. The two-storey, wooden structure was in operation from 1830 to 1955, and is now a museum.

The cliffs near Trout River, on the western edge of Newfoundland's Gros Morne National Park, look upon the Gulf of St. Lawrence.